Foreword

For anyone wanting to explore and study the Bible, be it just from an inquisitive point of view or as a new Christian wanting to get to grips with the Bible's teaching, this book will prove an invaluable asset to Bible study. The book deals briefly with issues of authorship and provides assurance as to the authority of scripture. Its clear overview of the two Testaments; the background information; and the concise résumé to each book of the Bible, produce a helpful book that will serve both young believers and mature Christians equally well.

Peter J. Dennis
CheckPoint Christian Youth Trust

Reading Your Bible

A Starter's Guide

by Gavin Childress and Audrey Dooley
Illustrated by Gill Wild

© **Day One Publications**
Ryelands Road Leominster HR6 8NZ
email: sales@dayone.co.uk
www.dayone.co.uk

UK Tel: 01568 613 740
Fax: 01568 611 473

EuropeTel: ++ 44 1568 613 740

United States Tel: 706 554 5907
or Toll Free: 1-8-morebooks

Canada Tel: 519 763 0339

ISBN: 1 903087 41 4

Design Wild Associates Ltd   **Tel:** 0208 715 9224
Illustration Gill Wild

Contents

Start here

The Bible you hold in your hand is very special. In fact there is no other book like it in the whole world. This book is inspired by God; the writers were guided by Him in every word they put on paper. In 2 Peter 1 we are told that holy men of God spoke as they were moved by the Holy Spirit.

The word "moved" means literally "carried along" and is the same word that is used in Acts 27:15 when the captain of a ship let the wind direct her: "we let her *drive*". God used their own experiences, their knowledge and styles of writing; yet He directed them.

Most of the books we have at home were written by just one person and took at most a year or two to finish. The Bible was written by about 40 people and took 2000 years to complete. It was written by kings, shepherds, fishermen, soldiers – even a doctor (Luke). It was written in different places: palaces, deserts, prisons, etc. Some parts were written during times of war, others during famine, and some in peacetime.

Some people say the Bible is so old, how can it speak to us today? It is indeed very old, yet man's sinful nature has not changed, and neither has our holy God. Therefore what the Bible has to teach us about ourselves, about our sin, and about the Lord Jesus Christ will never change. Jesus Christ came to teach us about God. He died on the cross to take away the punishment of sin. People of every age and background can be friends with God and live with Him forever.

If we were to look at the whole Bible as a library of God's teachings we would see the books like this:

LAW: They describe how God created the world and the laws which guided the Hebrews (His special people) to the promised land.

Law: GENESIS, EXODUS, LEVITICUS, NUMBERS, DEUTERONOMY

HISTORY: These books describe the history of God's people after they arrived at the promised land.

History: JOSHUA, JUDGES, RUTH, 1 SAMUEL, 2 SAMUEL, 1 KINGS, 2 KINGS, 1 CHRONICLES, 2 CHRONICLES, EZRA, NEHEMIAH, ESTHER

POETRY: Here are songs of praise and worship. There are many wise sayings here.

Poetry: JOB, PSALMS, PROVERBS, ECCLESIASTES, SONG OF SOLOMON

PROPHETS: These people "spoke out" God's word as well as foretelling the future. They warned against things like idolatry, injustice, and immorality. They also foretold that God would save and bless His people.

Prophecy: ISAIAH, JEREMIAH, LAMENTATIONS, EZEKIEL, DANIEL, HOSEA, JOEL, AMOS, OBADIAH, JONAH, MICAH, NAHUM, HABAKKUK, ZEPHANIAH, HAGGAI, ZECHARIAH, MALACHI

HISTORY: These books tell us about Jesus Christ and the early Christians.

History: MATTHEW, MARK, LUKE, JOHN, THE ACTS

LETTERS: These letters were mostly written by Paul to the early Christians as many people came to know about Jesus.

Letters: ROMANS, 1 CORINTHIANS, 2 CORINTHIANS, GALATIANS, EPHESIANS, PHILIPPIANS, COLOSSIANS, 1 THESSALONIANS, 2 THESSALONIANS, 1 TIMOTHY, 2 TIMOTHY, TITUS, PHILEMON, HEBREWS, JAMES, 1 PETER, 2 PETER, 1 JOHN, 2 JOHN, 3 JOHN, JUDE

PROPHECY: This book tells us much about future events.

Prophecy: REVELATION

Pick up your Bible

At first it may seem an enormous book to read. It may even be the largest book you have ever been given. Many Christians remember thinking they could never read through the whole Bible, and have since read it many times over. We have heard of a man who read it over 500 times, and have known people who manage to read the whole Bible every month! But the most important thing is to *understand* what you read, and for the Holy Spirit to speak to you as you read your Bible.

Look again at the Bible you hold in your hands. It is not really one book, but many books - 66 to be precise. It is a self-contained library that can be taken with you wherever you go. If it still seems too big, take heart; 24 of the books contain less than five chapters. Each of these books help us to know God. We need all of the books to know the will of God, and to understand what God is like. Later on we give a brief summary of each book to help you as you read your Bible. God did not give us His word to confuse us, but these books stand together to help us learn more about Him.
Let us explain how to find a verse in the Bible. If you see John 14:6 it means the gospel of John chapter 14, and the next part, ':6' means that once you have found the chapter you need to look up the small numbers among the words. These are the verses. Thus, John 14:6 means the gospel of John chapter 14 verse 6. (If you have problems finding a book in the Bible, look in the list of books near the front of the Bible to see the page number).

"Every word of God is pure" (Psalm 30:5).

Remember to pray before and during your study of the Bible. It is God who has given us this priceless treasure to show us His will, how to worship, how to serve and how to be friends with Him. We should therefore read it with great care, praying all

the time that God will speak to us. The Bible helps us so much when we read with an open heart. But if we read just to obtain knowledge or to impress our friends, our spiritual growth will be hindered.

Start at the beginning...

Open your Bible at the very beginning. After a few pages you will see a list of the books of the Bible like that opposite:

As we have seen, the Bible is basically a library of books to show us how to know God and to serve Him. You will notice that the first group is called "The Books of the Old Testament". This group is by far the largest, and all 39 of these books were written *before* Jesus Christ was born on the earth. The gap between the end of the Old Testament and the beginning of the New Testament is about 400 years.

The second group of books begins with Matthew and ends with Revelation. This section is called "The Books of the New Testament", and these books were written *after* Jesus Christ lived on the earth. They trace His life and the progress of Christianity throughout many parts of the world.

God has revealed His truth in the Bible in different forms of writing, such as laws and teachings. History books, for example Joshua and Judges, reveal His relationship with His people. He also speaks through poetry books, for instance Psalms and Proverbs, and through books of prophecy, such as Daniel, which foretell events far away in the future.

Old Testaments Books | New Testaments Books

	CHAPTERS		CHAPTERS
GENESIS	50	MATTHEW	28
Exodus	40	Mark	16
Leviticus	27	Luke	24
Numbers	36	John	21
Deuteronomy	34	The Acts	28
Joshua	24	Romans	16
Judges	21	1 Corinthians	16
Ruth	4	2 Corinthians	13
1 Samuel	31	Galatians	6
2 Samuel	24	Ephesians	6
1 Kings	22	Philippians	4
2 Kings	25	Colossians	4
1 Chronicles	29	1 Thessalonians	5
2 Chronicles	36	2 Thessalonians	3
Ezra	10	1 Timothy	6
Nehemiah	13	2 Timothy	4
Esther	10	Titus	3
Job	42	Philemon	1
Psalms	150	Hebrews	13
Proverbs	31	James	5
Ecclesiastes	12	1 Peter	5
Song of Solomon	8	2 Peter	3
Isaiah	66	1 John	5
Jeremiah	52	2 John	1
Lamentations	5	3 John	1
Ezekiel	48	Jude	1
Daniel	12	Revelation	22
Hosea	14		
Joel	3		
Amos	9		
Obadiah	1		
Jonah	4		
Micah	7		
Nahum	3		
Habakkuk	3		
Zephaniah	3		
Haggai	2		
Zechariah	14		
Malachi	4		

The Old Testament
Introduction

The Bible was originally written in two main languages, the Old Testament in Hebrew and the New Testament in Greek. Hebrew is a very expressive and colourful language, ideal for telling us about God and His dealings with His people. Greek is a language which can give us deep teaching in a very detailed and precise way. It is ideal for teaching people Christian doctrine. The New Testament mainly uses the common Greek of ordinary people to teach us. Greek was the language of much of the ancient world, and therefore perfect for the spread of the gospel all over the Middle East and Europe.

The Old Testament gives us the history of God's goodness to His people. It tells us about the Israelites, their triumphs and their failures. We can trace them from the time of Abraham (Genesis 12) who was told to leave his native city of Ur (in Iraq), and become a wanderer. His descendants went into Egypt where they eventually became slaves. After more than 400 years (Acts 7:6) God brought them out and led them to the land of Israel.

There, led by judges (such as Gideon and Samson) they had great victories against their enemies. Later, they wanted kings to rule them, and many times they rebelled against God. He sent them prophets who warned them of their sin. Eventually, God sent the Assyrians against them, who destroyed many cities and put great fear into the people. A long time afterwards, the Babylonians were sent to finally conquer Israel because of their sins. Most of the nation was taken captive to the land of Babylon, where they remained for 70 years (see Psalm 137).

A small number returned. They rebuilt Jerusalem and began to worship God again. More than ever, the Jews longed for a coming king, anointed by God—the Messiah, or Christ (see Isaiah 9:6). The Old Testament ends with God's people looking forward to His coming, and speaks about the work of John the Baptist who would pave the way for Him.

The New Testament

Introduction

The New Testament begins with the life and teaching of Jesus Christ in the four gospels: Matthew, Mark, Luke and John. These take us from the time of His birth to His ascension (when He went back to heaven). They show us what He taught and His many miracles. Jesus told His followers that after His ascension they were to wait in Jerusalem until the Holy Spirit came upon them with power. Then they were to tell people everywhere all about Him, beginning in Jerusalem, then in Judea and Samaria, and then to the ends of the earth (Acts 1:8). The record of their early missions is found in the Acts of the Apostles.

There follows, from 1 Corinthians onwards, many letters. These letters teach us about Christ, about Christian behaviour and doctrine. The last book of the Bible, the book of Revelation, teaches us about the future—times of great suffering as well as great joy. It also tells us about the second coming of Jesus and the glories of heaven.

Can we trust the Bible?

In 1947 a young Bedouin boy throwing stones into a cave made a startling discovery. He heard the sound of a clay jar breaking. When later the cave was searched there were found to be many such jars, all containing very old parchments. In all, eleven caves were found to contain thousands of fragments of the Word of God in Hebrew. The Dead Sea Scrolls had been uncovered, untouched for almost 19 centuries. These contained ancient copies of much of the Old Testament, some dating back to at least 200BC. Until then the earliest copies were

from about 900AD. They reveal that the Hebrew scriptures used in the Bible had been preserved with absolute care by the scribes who copied them.

There are so many New Testament manuscripts that Bible scholars have put them into groups. Some manuscripts vary from each other in small details. However, the early Christians wrote lots of helpful books which are not in the Bible. These are full of quotations from the earliest New Testament scrolls, including possibly original manuscripts. By piecing together these quotations we are able to reconstruct large sections of the New Testament. This has shown yet again just how much we can trust our Bibles.

The Bible has been wonderfully preserved through the ages. We do not have the original manuscripts of the books of the Bible but we must remember that the Jews were experts at copying the Word of God with great accuracy. Luke 24:27,44 shows us how completely our Lord Jesus believed in the truth and authority of the Old Testament, quoting from the whole range of inspired books. Paul also had complete confidence in the Old Testament (see Acts 24:14).

The Bible is complete, and no one must add or take away from it (see Deuteronomy 4:2, Proverbs 30:5-6, Revelation 22:18-19). Our task, as that of every generation, is to pass on the Bible in its entirety, with no verses missing or added, to our children and their children.

"So, where should I start reading?"

A good place to start is the New Testament. When you have finished that, then read through the Old Testament. The whole Bible is the Word of God, and all of it has been inspired by Him. The apostle Paul says, "All scripture is given by inspiration of God, and is profitable for doctrine, for reproof, for correction, for instruction in righteousness..." (2 Timothy 3:16).

It is important to read from the entire Bible, since it stands together as a whole. The New Testament tells us the most about Jesus Christ, and how to know and love Him; that is where we shall look now.

Matthew

Please open your Bible at the first book of the New Testament, the gospel according to Matthew. This is an excellent place to start reading, since this gospel frequently reminds us of its Old Testament background, encouraging us to look back through other parts of the Bible. We will concentrate on Matthew's gospel for a while and give you as much help as we can while you read it.

"Gospel" means "glad tidings", or "good news". The gospels tell us the good news about the coming of the Lord Jesus Christ into the world, how He lived, how He died and rose again. But they are even more special because they show us how we can know Jesus and how to serve Him. That is truly "good news!"

This is why we must read all four gospels to get a full picture of Jesus' life. Each gospel has a slightly different emphasis as it looks at the life of Jesus. All the gospels tell us about the teaching of John the Baptist, the baptism of Jesus, the time He fed 5,000 people, His triumphal entry into Jerusalem, His death and His resurrection. Only two gospels, Matthew and Luke, give us any detail about His birth.

The title of this gospel, like each of the other four, tells us who wrote it – Matthew. He had been a tax collector, (sometimes called a "publican"), which at that time was a job full of swindling and corruption. Yet Jesus saved him. You can read about how he left everything behind and followed Jesus in Matthew 9:9.

Matthew begins with a long list of names. This list proves that Jesus descended from king David and, further back, from Abraham. This gospel tells us about the birth of Jesus, and many details of His life and teaching which you will not find in the other gospels. None of the gospels tell us about the life of Jesus from the age of 12 to about 30, when His ministry began. All we know is that people called Him "the carpenter's son" (Matthew 13:55). The Lord called 12 men to be His followers, or "disciples", and He taught them in great detail about His purpose and mission.

Matthew chapters 5, 6 and 7 contain the Sermon on the Mount, where Jesus taught us how to be His true followers. Matthew tells us about many parables and miracles of the Lord Jesus. He tells us all about the "kingdom of heaven", a phrase you will only find in this gospel.

This gospel is particularly famous for the number of times it refers to the Old Testament. Jesus said and did many things which were foretold centuries before His life on earth. Below are some of the places in Matthew where the Old Testament is quoted. If you have time, look up the verses in both the Old and New Testaments. Matthew's gospel is summarised again later in this book.

Look up the verses below; first in Matthew's Gospel then in the Old Testament

If you feel you are too slow in looking up places in the Bible, don't worry. As you get to know the Bible you'll get faster.

Matthew	Old Testament
1:23	Isaiah 7:14
2:15	Hosea 11:1
2:17-18	Jeremiah 31:15
4:6	Psalm 91:11-12
4:7	Deuteronomy 6:16
4:15-16	Isaiah 9:1-2
9:13	Hosea 6:6
11:10	Malachi 3:1
12:3-4	1 Samuel 21:6
12:41	Jonah 3:5-9

Matthew	Old Testament
12:42	1 Kings 10:1
13:35	Psalm 78:2
15:4	Exodus 20:12
15:7-8	Isaiah 29:13
19:5	Genesis 2:24
19:7	Deuteronomy 24:1
21:16	Psalm 8:2
24:15	Daniel 9:27
26:67	Isaiah 50:6

A map of Matthew's gospel

It is very helpful, when reading the Bible, to know where the places are on a map. The map below shows us places Jesus visited during His ministry, as recorded in Matthew's gospel.

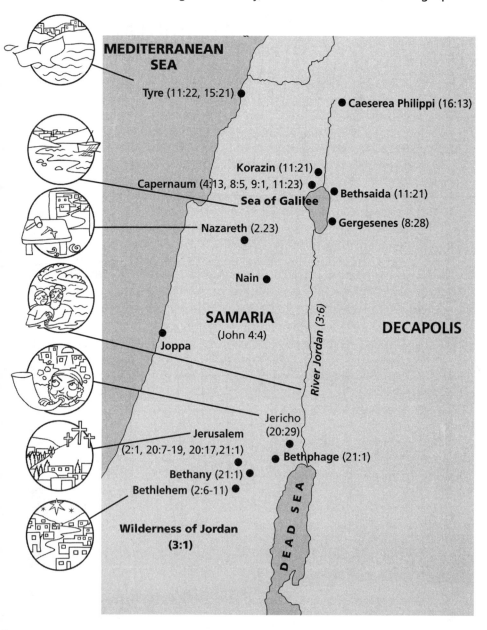

MEDITERRANEAN SEA

Tyre (11:22, 15:21)

Caeserea Philippi (16:13)

Korazin (11:21)

Capernaum (4:13, 8:5, 9:1, 11:23)

Sea of Galilee

Bethsaida (11:21)

Nazareth (2.23)

Gergesenes (8:28)

Nain

SAMARIA
(John 4:4)

River Jordan (3:6)

DECAPOLIS

Joppa

Jericho (20:29)

Jerusalem
(2:1, 20:7-19, 20:17,21:1)

Bethphage (21:1)

Bethany (21:1)

Bethlehem (2:6-11)

DEAD SEA

Wilderness of Jordan
(3:1)

There are three main seas on this map of Israel. On the left of the map you will see the Mediterranean Sea, which the Bible sometimes calls the Great Sea. It was here that Jonah was swallowed by a huge fish (see the book of Jonah, chapters 1 and 2).

Next is the Sea of Galilee (near the top of the map). It was in this area that Jesus grew up, and where He spent a lot of time during His three and a half year ministry. It was in view of this beautiful sea that He gave the Sermon on the Mount. Jesus instructed His disciples to go to meet Him in Galilee after His resurrection: "after I am risen again, I will go before you into Galilee" (Matthew 26:32).

Further down the map is the Dead Sea. It is called "dead" because no fish can live in its very salty water. The Dead Sea today covers the place where there was once some very wicked cities. You can read what happened to one of them, called Sodom, in Genesis 19:23-26. Just to the west of the Dead Sea you will notice some very important places, including Bethlehem – where Jesus was born (see Matthew 2:6-11 and Micah 5:2) – and also Jerusalem, the place where Jesus often preached and where He died on the cross, rose from the dead and ascended to heaven.

Between the Sea of Galilee and the Dead Sea you will notice the winding shape of the River Jordan. It was here that multitudes were baptized by John the Baptist, including Jesus Himself (see Matthew 3:13-17).

Just near the southern part of the River Jordan you will see Jericho. It was here that Joshua won his famous victory (Joshua 6:1-5).

You now know the main areas on the map. Almost every hill, valley and town has a Bible story associated with it. Keep this map near you as you read the gospel of Matthew. You will find that Jesus kept travelling back and forth between Galilee and Jerusalem during His ministry. In many ways He encountered the most opposition in His hometown of Nazareth, and in Jerusalem, the centre of religious life.

The Bible at a Glance

Now look at the first five books of the Bible: Genesis, Exodus, Leviticus, Numbers, Deuteronomy. These names may seem hard to understand at first, but once you know what they are about, it will be much easier. You may already know the meaning of two of them; Genesis means "beginnings" and Numbers means that the book tells us about the "numbers" of people who came out of Egypt when God set them free.

Take up your Bible again and open it in the middle. You should find here the book of Psalms (in fact the middle verse of the whole Bible is Psalm 118:8). The word "Psalms" just means "songs". The Psalms teach us about God's care, they praise Him and they warn us about sin.

If you turn towards the end of the Bible you will find the New Testament. This tells us about Jesus. It tells us what He and His followers did and what they taught.

We have seen that the Old Testament books were written before the coming of Jesus and the New Testament books afterwards.

* * * * * *

A Tour of the Bible

Introduction

Here is a very simplified look at the Old and New Testaments. The summaries that follow are intended to just give a flavour of what each book is about. Of course the best way to get to know the Bible is to read it through for yourself.

We have also tried to help the reader by grouping the books of the Bible into general sections, such as law, history and poetry. You will notice that the books of the Bible do not always follow each other in chronological order, but are grouped according to their subject matter and, in the case of the Prophets, their length.

It is very hard to give a brief summary of the Bible without overloading you with facts and figures. But here is a swift journey through the Bible. As you follow it, feel free to pause to take in what you have read. There are verses of the Bible you might wish to memorise, and these are set out for you in each section.

SECTION

1

LAW

Genesis

A text to remember: **Genesis 1:1-3**

The word Genesis means "beginnings" and this is a book which speaks of the beginning of creation right up to the beginning of the Hebrew nation. Look at the first chapter. It tells us that heaven and earth, and all that is in them were made by God. He was there right from the very beginning. It is not a book of myths but of real facts. Many books have been written which help us to see that the Bible and modern science are not in conflict. The great ages of the people who lived before the Flood remind us that we were originally created to live forever, but gradually the effect of sin shortened our lifespan to its present 70 years or so.

This book brings to life the hopes and fears of people just like ourselves, who lived many centuries ago. You probably already know a lot about it. It tells us about the worldwide Flood, the tower of Babel, the lives of Abraham, Isaac and Jacob. It also tells us the wonderful way that God guided and preserved Jacob's most famous son, Joseph.

The book of Genesis was written by Moses, as indeed were each of the first five books of the Bible.

Outline of book: Total chapters – 50

- God's beautiful creation – its beginning, fall into sin, destruction by flood, and re-population (1-11)

- God's call to Abraham, Isaac and Jacob (12-36)

- God saves the lives of Joseph and the Hebrew people (37-50)

Exodus

A text to remember: **Exodus 6:6,7**

Exodus sounds something like "exit", a way to get out. Here, Moses records the journey of the Hebrew people (the Israelites) as they escaped Egypt and their subsequent travels in a hot and dry wilderness. Moses, who was himself chosen by God for the task of leadership, tells us about the ten fearful plagues which fell upon the Egyptians. God freed His people and continued to protect, guide and teach them. Their final destination was to be the fruitful land of Canaan, a land promised by God to be given to Abraham's descendants.

Exodus hardly ever portrays the people of God as submissive and obedient. Indeed in many ways it is a record of their imperfections, despite the constant kindness of God. In chapter 20 we read of the time when God gave His people the Ten Commandments. God also gave them detailed plans of the tabernacle ("tent") where He was to be worshipped, and the many offerings and sacrifices that were to be made. The animals were killed to show that the only way our sins will ever be forgiven is if blood is spilled for us. The sacrifices were to be of perfect animals, and pointed to the truly sinless Lamb of God, the Lord Jesus Christ.

Outline of book: Total chapters – 40

- Israelites – in Egypt and their departure (1-14)
- Israelites – in the wilderness *Part 1* (15-40). The second part is in Numbers

Leviticus

A text to remember: **Leviticus 19:2**

This book is all about the various offerings and ceremonies which were necessary at that time for a believer to serve God. "Leviticus" has its name because God's priests came from a tribe called Levi, and the book is all about the various sacrifices which the priests and the people had to make for God.

It also contains many more general laws, including the first appearance of the well-known command to love your neighbour as yourself (chapter 19:18).

It was intended for the Levites to supervise these commands and serve God in the Tabernacle. Aaron, (Moses' brother), and his descendants were to be "high priests" and ultimately mediate between God and the people. Now Christ has become our High Priest and prays to the Father for His people.

This book tells us in chapters 13 and 14 how leprosy can be detected and how a leper can be made clean. Chapter 18 tells us who we can and cannot marry in our families. Notice how many detailed ceremonies and sacrifices had to be performed, some daily. They were fulfilled when Jesus came as the *perfect sacrifice*, and have therefore been "abolished". (Ephesians 2:14-16).

Outline of book: Total chapters – 27)

- ■ Sacrifices, offerings, and priests are set in place for God's worship (1-10)

- ■ Various laws and holy days are established for the Israelite people (11-27)

Numbers

A text to remember: **Numbers 14:8,9**

As its name suggests, this is a book which tells us the "numbers" of male Israelites who left Egypt and were aged 20 and over (see chapter 1:45,46) and later "numbers" of people as they camped near the promised land (chapter 26). However this book contains much more. It also records the "numbers" of those who rebelled against God.

It tells us about how the Israelites doubted God time after time, especially in chapters 13 and 14 with their refusal to enter the promised land of "Canaan" (afterwards named Israel). They then had to wander in the desert for 40 years, until that whole rebellious generation had died, before God permitted them to enter the beautiful promised land. Only two faithful men of that generation, Joshua and Caleb, were permitted to enter the land. Psalm 78 and 106 outline just how far God's people rebelled during this period.

Outline of book: Total chapters – 36

■ Israelites – numbered and worship begins (1-9)

■ Israelites – in the wilderness *Part 2* (10-36)

Deuteronomy

A text to remember: **Deuteronomy 6:4,5**

Deuteronomy sounds complicated, but it gets easier once you know that "nomos" means law. Deuteronomy is the "Second telling of the Law".

This book is therefore a powerful reminder of the laws already given by God to the Israelites. Moses is the writer and here speaks at length to the elders and people shortly before his death and their entry into Canaan. Turn to chapter 5 and you will find that the Ten Commandments are restated, as are many other laws.

Moses, throughout this book, constantly encourages the nation to obey God. They are reminded of God's provision, guidance and protection during their 40 years of travel in the wilderness. The poetic and powerful style shows sin to be very wicked and foolish, and God's law very sweet (see chapter 6:1-16 and chapter 32). Note the goodness and severity of God in chapter 28, where there are untold blessings for obedience and fearful curses for sin.

Outline of book: Total chapters – 34

- Moses – *remembers* the Israelites' past and restates Gods laws (1-26)

- Moses – *records* God's law and exhorts to obedience (27-30)

- Moses – his final instructions, song and death (31-34)

Joshua

A text to remember: **Joshua 24:15**

Joshua had been chosen as Moses' successor to lead the Israelite people triumphantly into the promised land (Canaan). He was one of the original spies who had seen Canaan 40 years earlier and was a man of great trust in God.

This book takes us from the time when Joshua entered Canaan to the dividing up of the land between the 12 tribes of God's people. Many battles were fought because God gave the land to the Jewish people and commanded them to drive out the original inhabitants. Chapter 6, for example, tells us of the famous fall of Jericho. God had commanded His people to enter and possess the land, but it had to be won by tough battles and great faith. Joshua learnt to trust in the God who promised never to leave him or forsake him (Joshua 1:5).

The kingdom of Jesus Christ now extends by love, not the sword (Matthew 26:52, John 18:36).

Outline of book: Total chapters – 24

- Joshua prepares to enter Canaan (1-2)
- The fight for Canaan (3-12)
- The division of Canaan (13-22)
- Joshua's final speech and death (23-24)

Judges

A text to remember: **Judges 2:12**

God's people were ruled at this time not by kings but judges. These were military leaders who performed heroic feats by the power of God. Almost all the judges sincerely loved the Lord, whereas most of the kings, who came later, were idolaters and wicked.

Many of the judges are famous to this day. Glance at Hebrews 11:32-40 and you will be introduced to four of the leaders who you will read about in this book: Gideon, Barak, Samson and Jephthah. Gideon is especially remembered for using a fleece to test God's will. Samson is remembered for his amazing strength!

We learn so much from the rugged godliness of these men and women of the past. Remember that although they were regarded as heroes, their faults are clearly recorded.

The period during which the judges ruled was a time of unrest. Time after time the Israelites forsook God's laws. The Bible blames the wickedness of God's people as the root cause for their sorrows (see chapter 4:1,2; 6:1 and 13:1).

Outline of book: Total chapters – 21

- Overview – failure of Israel to secure Canaan after Joshua's death (1-2)
- The lives of the judges of Israel (3-16)
- The sins of Israel – two accounts (17-21)

Ruth

A text to remember: **Ruth 1:16,17**

This book teaches us about a young woman named Ruth who, though from the pagan land of Moab, believed in the God of the Bible. After the death of her husband she followed her mother-in-law to the land of Israel. She settled in Bethlehem and married Boaz, a kind and spiritually minded man. Ruth was blessed by becoming the great-grandmother of king David and thus part of the lineage of Jesus Christ.

Ruth is a book packed full of the themes of love, loyalty and unselfishness. Almost without realising it the reader is here transported to an ancient world and gets a feel of day-to-day life in biblical times.

Outline of book: Total chapters – 4

- Grief in Moab. Naomi returns to Bethlehem with Ruth (1)
- Ruth works for Boaz (2)
- Ruth marries Boaz (3-4)

1 Samuel

A text to remember: **1 Samuel 17:45**

In this book we meet *Samuel*, and discover how he came to be chosen as a prophet and judge even from his boyhood.

1 and 2 Samuel cover the period from the last judges of Israel to the era of kings in Israel. 1 Samuel tells us about the anointing of Saul – their first king. The Israelites were meant only to have judges to rule them, not kings, because God was their true king.

Saul, the first king, was a man who stood physically head and shoulders above everyone else. He began his reign well. Yet later he fell away from the path of true holiness and was possessed by an evil spirit; see chapter 16:14.

David, was chosen by God to be the next king. We read in chapter 17 how David, firing just one sling-stone, famously defeated the arrogant Philistine giant Goliath. Much of the rest of the book shows us David's loyalty to Saul, and Saul's hatred of David. Many of David's Psalms were written during this period as he tried to hide from Saul (see Psalm 18, 54, 57, 59).

Outline of book: Total chapters – 31

- Samuel – The prophet and judge (1-12)
- Saul – The first king of Israel (13-15)
- David – His anointing as king and flight from Saul (16-30)
- The death of king Saul and his sons (31)

2 Samuel

A text to remember: **2 Samuel 1:27**

This book continues the narrative of the period of the kings with the ascension to the throne of king David and his victories over the surrounding nations. David has a heart for God and is blessed with the promise that his family will be great. It is from his family line that the "King of kings" – the Lord Jesus Christ – is descended.

The honesty and reliability of God's Word is clearly seen in this book. David the hero of the Jews commits adultery and murder in chapter 11. He is sternly rebuked by God, and later wrote his psalm of repentance, Psalm 51. His sin was forgiven, but violence would never depart from his household. We read in this book of many enemies of David, both inside and outside the ranks of his own men.

In chapter 14 onwards his own son, Absalom, begins to lead a conspiracy against him, and is later killed by Joab, David's General. It is a book that teaches us that God is merciful and kind toward those who truly love Him, and that He protects them.

Outline of book: Total chapters – 24

- ■ The reign of king David – Israel's mightiest king (1-10)
- ■ Trouble in David's household (11-19)
- ■ Trouble in David's kingdom (20-24)

1 Kings

A text to remember: **1 Kings 18:21**

David, being a man of war and bloodshed, was not allowed to build a temple for God. This was left to his wise son, Solomon, to perform. The special place of God's worship had been a tent or tabernacle since the days of Moses. Now it was time to construct a beautiful, permanent structure in which the worship of God could be performed. Solomon loved God and was very wealthy and wise. But it was his wives, not his wealth that took him away from God (chapter 11). After his death, his son Rehoboam made such a bad job of his reign that the people of Israel divided in two. The northern ten tribes left Rehoboam and kept the name *Israel*, whereas the southern two tribes became known as *Judah*.

Chapter 17 begins with the sudden appearance of the rugged prophet Elijah. He continually conflicts with the idolatrous and wicked king Ahab and his cruel wife Jezebel. The struggle between the pure worship of God and the false worship of the idol Baal is seen most vividly when he calls the people to come to Mount Carmel (chapter 18). Here Elijah calls upon God to send down fire, and tells the prophets of Baal to ask their false god to do the same. The result is clear!

Outline of book: Total chapters – 22

- The reign of king Solomon – Israel's wisest king (1-11)
- The kingdom is divided – Judah and Israel (12-22)
- The prophet Elijah's remarkable life (17-2 Kings 2)

2 Kings

A text to remember: **2 Kings 23:27**

This book begins at the time that Elijah and Elisha worked side by side as prophets of God. Here we see Elijah going up to heaven in a whirlwind and Elisha remaining on earth to serve God. The book shows us good kings, such as Asa, Hezekiah and especially Josiah. It also reveals a multitude of wicked kings such as Jeroboam and Zedekiah. Note how the spiritual strength or weakness of the king affected the entire nation. If he served God, so did the people; if he was an idolater, they too fell into sin. Note also that the people of God were now divided into two main groups: Israel and Judah (see 1 Kings). The kings in the north (Israel) reigned in Samaria, and those in the South (Judah) reigned in Jerusalem. Thus in chapter 17:1, Ahaz reigned in Judah at the same time as Hoshea in Israel. As you read, ask yourself, "Were all the *good* kings from Judah?"

Sadly, the continuing idolatry of the kings and people of Israel and Judah eventually led to God's judgment. First the Assyrians, then the Babylonians came and took multitudes captive as slaves to their own lands.

Outline of book: Total chapters – 25

- Countdown to Israel's captivity in Assyria (1-17)
- Remarkable lives of Elijah
  (1 Kings 17-2 Kings 2) and Elisha (1 Kings19-2 Kings13)
- Countdown to Judah's captivity in Babylon (18-25)

1 Chronicles

A text to remember: **1 Chronicles 4:10**

Family trees were very important to God's people in Bible times, as they proved the true descent of Jewish people. This book begins with the longest list of names in the whole Bible. It spans most of the first 12 chapters. Lists like these are very helpful for Bible students to see at a glance the various people in the Bible and how they are related. Note the occasions when the list of names stops for a moment and we learn more about a particular individual. One example is Jabez (see above verse). Note how one brief prayer changed the entire course of this man's life.

The rest of the book traces the life of King David right up to the time when his son Solomon became king. Much of what we read here has been given in 2 Samuel and 1 Kings. Similarly, 2 Chronicles contains much material from 1 and 2 Kings. This sort of repetition occurs mainly here and in the gospels. Clearly God wants us to especially remember these events.

Outline of book: Total chapters – 29

■ Family Trees (1-9)

■ David's kingdom and reign (10-29)

2 Chronicles

A text to remember: **2 Chronicles 14:11**

This book continues from the reign of Solomon and tells us about the various kings of Israel and Judah. 2 Chronicles especially concentrates on the biographies of the kings of *Judah* and says a lot about the faith of those kings who really trusted God. Look up these verses and read about the "good" kings who are here speaking: Asa (14:11), Jehoshaphat (20:21), Hezekiah (32:7,8) and Josiah (34:31).

Note again that much of this material is also found in 1 and 2 Kings. Sometimes events are recorded several times in the Bible. For example, when King Hezekiah became sick and prayed to God he was wonderfully healed. The prophet Isaiah lived at the same time and so spoke of it in his book. Compare what the Bible says about this event in 2 Chronicles 32:24-26, 2 Kings 20:1-11 and Isaiah 38.

Outline of book: Total chapters – 36

- Records relating to Solomon's kingdom and reign (1-9)
- Records relating to the kings of Judah and Israel (10-36)

Ezra

A text to remember: **Ezra 3:11**

The Jews who returned from Babylon had the emperor Cyrus of Persia on their side. But more importantly, God was with them. Their forefathers had left Jerusalem when the Babylonians had destroyed it. Now they were returning under the leadership of Zerubbabel and Ezra to build the temple again. Ezra, a scribe of God not mentioned until chapter 7, tells us frankly of the joys and hardships of rebuilding the temple. The people had become spiritually very lazy and cold and there was much opposition from their neighbours. This book tells us how the true service of God was re-established in Jerusalem. Haggai and Zechariah were the prophets sent to stir His people into action.

Outline of book: Total chapters – 10

- The first return to Jerusalem under Zerubbabel's leadership.

- God's temple is rebuilt (1-6)

- The second return to Jerusalem (80 years later) under Ezra's leadership – Ezra's nationwide reforms (7-10)

Nehemiah

A text to remember: **Nehemiah 9:6**

Nehemiah was a Jewish "cupbearer" to the Persian king Artaxerxes. When Nehemiah heard of the terrible state of Jerusalem, he prayed to God and was freed to go and rebuild the city. This book shows us the wonderful unity and zeal that the Jews had in repairing the ruined walls. Chapter 3 tells us who took part in the great task of reconstruction. Note in 3:12 that women helped rebuild too. Local officials, Sanballat and Tobiah, tried to stop the people working and discouraged them by all manner of schemes (chapter 4).

Nehemiah joined with Ezra in reading God's law to the people (chapter 8), and in encouraging the people to be pure. Nehemiah set about reforming the people so that their sins were put away. In chapter 5 we find that the 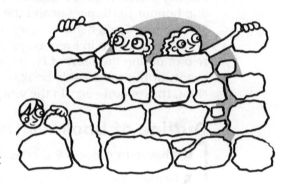 Israelites had lent money to each other at interest (usury). This was forbidden by the law of Moses. They had also intermarried with those who disregarded God and had broken the sabbath, i.e. by buying and selling on God's holy day (see chapter 13). Nehemiah hated all sin, and God blessed his efforts to restore the pure worship of God.

Outline of book: Total chapters – 13

- Third return to Jerusalem under Nehemiah's leadership - city walls are rebuilt (1-7)

- Re-dedication of people to God's laws. Nehemiah's nationwide reforms (8-13)

Esther

A text to remember: **Esther 4:13,14**

This book starts with a quarrel and ends in triumph. The Persian king Ahasuerus (also known as Xerxes) divorces his wife and seeks a new companion. Beautiful Esther is chosen from among hundreds of candidates. This wise Jewish woman with the help and guidance of God prevents the worldwide massacre of the Jews, planned by wicked Haman. There are four central figures: powerful king Ahasuerus, his wife Esther, her cousin Mordecai and the jealous royal official Haman.

In this book we clearly see God at work in every chapter, moving events toward a glorious finale which brings freedom and honour to His people and the overthrow of His enemies. Surprisingly, God's name is never mentioned in Esther, yet His providence is seen in every page. Jews today continue to rejoice during the feast of Purim, as each year they recall the events of this remarkable book.

Note: the longest verse in the whole Bible is Esther 8:9.

Outline of book: Total chapters – 10

- ■ Ahasuerus chooses Esther as queen (1-2)
- ■ Haman plans to destroy all Jews (3-4)
- ■ Esther and Mordecai plan to save the Jews (5-7)
- ■ The Jews are honoured. Their victory (8-10)

SECTION

3

POETRY

Job

A text to remember: **Job 1:20-22**

Job is a book that probably describes our worst nightmare. Job loses everything in one foul swoop – family, possessions, even his health. Job was an outstandingly holy man. As a test of his faith the devil was permitted to rob Job of everything dear to him. At the end of the book God restores to Job double what Satan took away.

This book deals with the question of *why* bad things happen to seemingly "good" people. Job's friends visit him and offer him words of "consolation". In fact they accuse Job of hidden sin.

In the closing chapters, we see that God is the sovereign creator. He is in control of *all* things and answers to no one. He will indeed work "all things together for good to those who love God" (Romans 8:28).

Job is perhaps the first Bible book ever written. Look carefully at the beginning of the chapters to see who is speaking. If it is a friend of Job beware, because God rebukes their speeches at the end of the book (42:7). In 19:25,26 Job declares his faith both in his Redeemer (pointing to Jesus) and the fact of the resurrection of the body after death.

Outline of book: Total chapters – 42

- Job's distress (1-2)
- Job and his three friends reason together (3-31)
- Elihu reproves Job and his three companions (32-37)
- God speaks (38-42)

Psalms

A text to remember: Psalm 23

The Psalms are basically "songs" which are used to praise God. Ephesians 5:19 teaches us that Christians should still sing the Psalms. You will notice that a lot of what is said looks at *history, creation* and the *individual experiences* of the psalmists. Psalm 90 is a prayer of Moses. About 73 psalms are specifically attributed to King David. In Acts 1:16 Peter emphasises that the psalmist David spoke by the Holy Spirit. His best-known song is Psalm 23, where we are shown what good care God takes of His people, as a shepherd looks after his sheep.

Look carefully at the small titles to see the circumstances in which the psalms were written. Some psalms speak at length about the worries and problems of the writers, teaching us that we must never be false when we come before God, but bring to Him our problems and cares. Many psalms are full to the brim with adoration and worship. Some psalms speak directly about the Lord Jesus, and are called Messianic (See 2, 22, 31, 34, 45, 69, 110.). He himself drew attention to them (Luke 24:44).

The word "selah" occurs frequently and may mean a pause or a shout of triumph. Note that Psalms 146-150 begin and end with "Hallelujah", which in English means, "Praise the LORD".

Outline of book: Total chapters – 150

- *Some* Psalms of praise (8, 18, 30, 103, 145-150)
- *Some* Psalms when in trouble and afraid (13, 17, 27, 37, 54, 56, 64, 77, 88, 120, 140)
- *Some* Psalms of worship and hope (16, 19, 43, 46, 47, 48, 51, 56, 66, 91, 113, 121)

Proverbs

A text to remember: **Proverbs 1:7**

These are clear, sound practical words of wisdom, most of which were spoken by the wisest king of Israel, Solomon. He directs us to holiness in relationships, business, leisure etc. If we neglect this book, we will be the poorer for it.

This book is a warning to the idle and an encouragement to the hardworking. It exalts the fear of God as "the beginning of knowledge" and denounces evil and foolishness. Here nothing is taken for granted, because Solomon knew to his cost how powerful sin can be. Chapter 31 famously speaks of the wise and virtuous woman. Read this whole book prayerfully and its fruit will be seen in your life.

Outline of book: Total chapters – 31

■ Solomon's proverbs (1-29)

Look out for certain themes, such as:

a) the fear of God and gaining wisdom
   (1, 2, 3:7,13-20; 4:5-7; 5:1-2; 7:1-5, 8; 9:1-12;
   15:33; 16:16; 19:23; 22:4);

b) the righteous compared to the foolish
   (10:23-25; 13:20; 14:7-9; 16; 24:16; 28:1,5; 29:7,11);

c) avoiding strife
   (10:12; 15:1; 17:1,14; 25:8; 26:17; 26:20; 29:22)

d) giving freely to the poor
   (11:24,25; 13:7; 19:17; 21:26; 22:9; 28:27; 29:7; 31:20)

■ Agur's wise words (30)

■ Lemuel's wise words (31)

Ecclesiastes

A text to remember: **Ecclesiastes 12:1**

What is the point of life? To anyone who has ever considered this question we would recommend that they read this book and follow the reasoning of Solomon, the "Preacher". Solomon himself had tasted almost every pleasure this world has to offer. He describes the vast riches and greatness of his kingdom in chapter 2, and all the delightful pleasures he pursued to the full. Yet he sees that everything is truly vanity. There is emptiness everywhere under the sun. Solomon, a man who was wealthy, creative and hardworking tells us these things could not satisfy him. For those who are intrigued by the glitter and glamour of this world, he gives us the best sermon we could possibly hear. Chapter 3 is very well known as it speaks of a time for everything: "a time to be born, and a time to die..."

Some see this book as very negative; but it is written as an antidote to sin and foolishness. It is written to sober us up to see that this world and all that is in it is passing away. He tells us to consider death (7:2) and to remember our Creator while we are still young (12:1).

Solomon concludes that the greatest way to live is not for pleasure or anything else, but to fear God and keep His commandments (12:13). Without God "all is vanity".

Outline of book: Total chapters – 12

- Solomon pursues fulfilment in wisdom, pleasure, creativity and hard work (1-2)
- Solomon's observations of life in this world (3-11)
- Solomon's advice to the young and conclusion (12)

Song of Solomon

A text to remember: **Song of Solomon 5:16**

No two books are in greater contrast than Ecclesiastes and the Song of Solomon. Yet the same man wrote them both, guided as he was by the Holy Spirit. Ecclesiastes taught us the vanity of this world's pleasures. The Song of Solomon teaches us the importance of true love. It speaks at one level of Solomon and his bride, but at a deeper level of the relationship between Christ and His people. You will see very similar language in Isaiah 5:1-7 and Psalm 45. This Psalm is all about the beauty of Christ (see Hebrews 1:8,9) and His bride the church.

The study of this book is greatly helped when you know who is speaking. Clues in the original Hebrew have enabled Bible scholars to tell whether the person referred to is male or female, singular or plural. We would recommend you take the time to mark your Bible as you can see below. Ask the Holy Spirit to speak to you from the glorious pages of this love song.

Outline of book: Total chapters – 8

(Note: 'a' is the first part of the verse and 'b' the second part. Thus '8:5a' means the first part of chapter 8 verse 5)

■ Bride speaking:
[1:1-7, 12-14, 16] [2:3-10a, 16-17] [3:1-11] [4:16]
[5:2a, 3-8, 10-16] [6:2-3] [7:10-13] [8:1-4, 5b-7, 10-14]

■ Bridegroom speaking:
[1:8-11, 15, 17] [2:1-2, 10b-15] [4:1-15] [5:1, 2b]
[6:4-13] [7:1-9]

■ Friends speaking:
[5:9] [6:1] [8:5a, 8-9]

Isaiah

A text to remember: **Isaiah 9:6**

This book tells us a great deal about the kingdom of our Lord Jesus Christ. If you read chapters 7:14, 9:6-7, 40 and 53 you will see that they speak directly about Him. This book, along with the Psalms, is quoted most in the New Testament. We have here an example of the full spectrum of biblical prophecy. This is seen in the balance between *history* and *allegory*, *fearful judgments* and *wonderful blessings*.

Isaiah ends by describing the future glory of God's kingdom when there will be new heavens and a new earth. The book is full of powerful imagery. Chapter 6 describes Isaiah's vision of the Lord as "high and lifted up", and of his own awareness of sin. What a remarkable sight of God he had on the day that he was called to be a prophet!

Today, many people make the choice between a faith that emphasises social action, and a faith that focuses on our devotion to God. Yet both are vital. Chapter 58 speaks of the importance of justice for the oppressed (verse 6) and balances this with the importance of God's worship. The chapter ends by speaking of the Sabbath day, and tells us that those who delight to give God one day in seven in effect delight in *Him* (58:13,14).

Outline of book: Total chapters – 66

- The visions and prophecies of Isaiah – calls to repentance, and warnings of judgment to Judah and many nations. A remnant will be saved (1-35)

- Isaiah and king Hezekiah (36-39)

- The salvation of God's people, who are drawn from all nations (40-66)

Jeremiah

A text to remember: **Jeremiah 17:5**

Imagine having the most vital and urgent message in the world, and no one wants to listen! This was the great burden of the life of Jeremiah. For this reason he is known as the weeping prophet. God's judgment would begin with His own people. He called upon the people of Judah to repent and return to God before the Babylonians came and took away all that God's people had built up. The Babylonians (from modern-day Iraq) had built an empire, and wanted to expand their territory by conquest and slave labour. Like Isaiah, this book also speaks of God's judgment upon the surrounding nations. Unlike Isaiah, the message contains far more about judgment than blessing. Eventually, God saw to it that the Babylonians destroyed Jerusalem with all of its wealth and its glorious temple. The book ends with the people taken captive to Babylon. Imprisoned several times for his words of warning, Jeremiah had the unenviable task of warning a deaf and hard-hearted people.

Outline of book: Total chapters – 52

- The visions and prophecies of Jeremiah – calls to repentance and warnings of judgment to *Judah*. A remnant will be saved (1-45)

- The visions and prophecies of Jeremiah – calls to repentance and warnings of judgment to *surrounding nations* (46-51)

- The captivity of Judah by the Babylonians (52)

Lamentations

A text to remember: **Lamentations 3:22,23**

If you ever wondered what life was like for those left behind when the Babylonians had ransacked Jerusalem, this book answers your question. Images from this book of hungry children and emaciated youths stay with us. Yet in the midst of these terrible judgments, God is still merciful. God's great faithfulness shines through the gloom (see above verses). Chapter 3 reveals much of the message of the book—a faithful God, an unfaithful people and the misery of sin's consequences.

Outline of book: Total chapters – 5

- ■ Judah's sorrow *Part 1* (1-2)
- ■ Jeremiah's own *sorrow* (3)
- ■ Judah's sorrow *Part 2* (4-5)

Ezekiel

A text to remember: **Ezekiel 11:19,20**

Ezekiel was a priest among the Jewish captives in Babylon. As he stood by the river Chebar, he had a wonderful vision of God's glory and the living creatures that serve Him. As in Isaiah 6, Ezekiel's call from God was certainly dramatic. Yet, like Jeremiah, Ezekiel had the hard task of preaching to people who didn't want to know (3:1-8). He was told, however, of the importance of warning the wicked of judgment even if they refused to hear (chapters 3 and 18).

Ezekiel saw many visions of God's glory and of His judgment. His vision of the valley of dry bones (chapter 37) is well known, and teaches that God would raise up His people again from their misery and apparent "death". The book ends with visions of God's spiritual temple and the living waters of His holy city.

Outline of book: Total chapters – 48

- Ezekiel – his initial visions, calling and commission (1-3)
- Further visions, prophecies and parables against Israel and Judah (4-24)
- Prophecies concerning other nations (25-35, 38-39)
- Promises of future restoration (36-37)
- Visions of God's spiritual temple and land (40-48)

Daniel

A text to remember: **Daniel 7:14**

This book tells us about life in Babylon for the captive Jews, and reveals that God had not abandoned them. He was at work protecting and blessing the Jewish people. Daniel and his friends refused to eat food offered to idols. They stood firm for God wherever they were instead of giving way and compromising. Shadrach, Meshach and Abednego refused to bow to wicked king Nebuchadnezzar's image; therefore they were cast into a burning fiery furnace (chapter 3). Yet God preserved them alive. He also protected Daniel when he was thrown into a den of lions (chapter 6).

The second part of the book is full of symbols and imagery. This book is called "apocalyptic", as is the book of Revelation (which you will find at the end of the Bible). That means, it reveals events far into the future. Thus the book of Daniel talks about the coming of the Messiah (9:26, etc). It speaks of the rise and fall of empires, describing them as, for instance, parts of a statue of a man (chapter 2) or as ferocious animals (chapter 7) etc. These visions point us ultimately to a kingdom which will never die; the eternal kingdom of the Messiah (see 2:44 and 7:13,14).

Later the book speaks of the resurrection of the dead when everyone will stand before God (12:2,3). Don't worry that so much of this book is mysterious, and hard to understand. Daniel himself did not always know the meaning of what was shown to him (12:8); but he wrote his visions down so that as these events take place readers would realise it and seek God.

Outline of book: Total chapters – 12

- Daniel and friends triumph despite evils and persecutions in Babylon (1-6)

- Daniel interprets mysterious dreams and signs (2,4 and 5)

- Daniel's prophetic visions (7-12)

Hosea

A text to remember: **Hosea 3:5**

Although Hosea lived *before* Isaiah's time, this book comes later in the Bible because it is shorter. The books of Isaiah to Daniel are known as the "major prophets" and Hosea onwards are called the "minor prophets". This is not because they are less important, but simply because their books are shorter.

In this book, God is angry with His people because of their idolatry and backsliding (see 4:16,17; 6:4; 10:13 etc.). Hosea himself is told to find a wife who was unfaithful, because this is what the people had done to God. He was as a husband to them, and they had committed spiritual adultery. Yet there is still hope for the people, for one day they would return to God (3:5).

Outline of book: Total chapters – 14

■ Hosea marries a sinful wife to show how Israel have treated God (their spiritual husband) (1-3)

■ Hosea speaks of forthcoming judgment and holds out promises of God's abundant mercy (4-14)

Joel

A text to remember: **Joel 2:12,13**

God punishes sin, yet is also full of compassion. This book speaks of the immediate judgments of God for sin, yet also the great mercy of God toward His people.

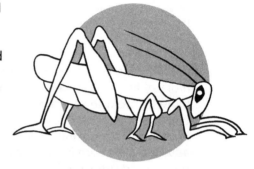

A terrible famine had come upon the land, as crops were destroyed by swarms of insects (1:4). This symbolised the judgment of God. Joel speaks of the great and fearful "day of the Lord". In 2:12-17 we see the importance of repentance not only about our own personal sins, but the sins of the nation. The priests were told to weep and cry out to God for mercy.

Later, we read of the tremendous blessings God's people would one day enjoy, as He restores what the locust had eaten (2:25). In the last days the Holy Spirit would be poured upon the people (see 2:28-32 and the fulfilment in Acts 2:16-21). Chapter 3:18 refers not only to the abundant harvests, but also the spiritual blessings of Christ's eternal kingdom.

Outline of book: Total chapters – 3

- Joel describes days of famine and desolation *after* God's judgments (1)
- Joel warns of the "day of the LORD" and judgment (2-3)

Amos

A text to remember: **Amos 5:4**

Amos was a herdsman. He was called, like Elisha, to leave his flock and become a prophet. As with earlier prophets, Amos turns his eyes toward a number of surrounding nations and warns of judgment. He warns them that fire will consume their palaces, showing that the rulers will especially be held accountable for their sins. Then in chapter 2:4 attention is drawn to Judah. The people of God will have to face God's judgment as well. Chapter 9:2-6 could not be expressed more powerfully—if God is angry with you, there is nowhere to hide. Chapter 6 warns that God's people had become complacent and relaxed. They had to be stirred up to serve God again. Chapter 8:11 tells us the worst famine of all is when we are deprived of the words of the Lord. The book ends in a similar way to Joel, speaking in beautiful language of the coming fruitfulness of the Messiah's kingdom.

Outline of book: Total chapters – 9

- God's wrath against the nations (1-2:3)
- God's anger against Judah and Israel. Restoration promised (2:4-9)

Obadiah

A text to remember: **Obadiah v. 4**

Only one chapter long, this book speaks about the people of Edom who were descendants of Esau, Jacob's brother. They were therefore related to the Israelites, and should have been loyal. However, they had joined hands with those who fought against Israel. God would therefore punish them for their sin (verse 15). Their land would one day be in the hands of God's people (verses 19-20) and the Lord Himself would rule them.

Outline of book: Total chapters – 1

- Edom's pride is revealed (vv. 1-9)

- Edom's foolishness in joining others to destroy Jacob [Israel] is condemned (vv. 10-14)

- Edom's downfall versus Israel's triumph (vv. 15-21)

Jonah

A text to remember: **Jonah 2:9**

Words fail us to describe the ancient cruelty of the Assyrians. They ruled a huge empire in what we now call Iran, and hardly ever lost a battle. They had no sympathy toward women, children or the elderly. They thought nothing of mutilating their prisoners, and rejoiced in their wickedness. Nineveh was their well-fortified capital city. Jonah, a prophet also referred to in 2 Kings 14:25, was called by God to go and warn the people of Nineveh that God was angry with them.

Jonah, who both feared and hated the Assyrians, took a ship to Tarshish (Spain) instead. A storm came and Jonah was thrown overboard. God, who governs all His creatures, prepared a big fish to swallow  Jonah. In chapter 2 we find him praying to God and recognising that "salvation is of the Lord" (2:9). God was merciful and called him a second time (3:1-2), and remarkably the people of Nineveh repented. Jonah was angry with God for sending him to these wicked people, only to show mercy to them later.

It is a book that teaches the wonderful mercy and power of God. It also warns us of the dangers of disobedience and hard-heartedness.

Outline of book: Total chapters – 4

- ■ Jonah disobeys God, and suffers the consequences (1)
- ■ Jonah's prayer and deliverance (2)
- ■ Jonah preaches in Nineveh – the people repent (3)
- ■ Jonah's anger (4)

Micah

A text to remember: **Micah 5:2**

As in the book of Amos, God's people had become secure in their sinful lifestyle (see 2:1,2 and 3:10,11). In chapter 1 God reminds the people of Samaria and Jerusalem that He has absolute power to punish them. In 4:10 God warns them that they will be taken captive to Babylon.

However, this book looks much further than simply immediate judgment. In chapter 5:2 it speaks of the future birth of Jesus in Bethlehem and of His kingdom. In chapter 7:18-20 it speaks of the great mercy and compassion of God toward His rebellious people. God is willing  to subdue their sin and forgive them again. How great is the mercy of God! He will "cast all their sins into the depths of the sea" (7:19).

Outline of book: Total chapters – 7

■ Micah warns of God's judgment (1-3)

■ Micah's prophecies of Christ's kingdom (4-5)

■ God's requirements of man (6-7)

Nahum

A text to remember: **Nahum 1:7**

In the book of Jonah, we read about the remarkable repentance of the people of Nineveh. In Nahum, however, we see that a later generation in that city turned back to their old sins. Nineveh, the city of blood (3:1) would be "laid waste" (3:7). It was destroyed in 606 BC, over 140 years after Jonah had preached in its streets. As with the book of Micah, so

here the glory of God is seen in the first chapter: "the clouds are the dust of His feet" (1:3). This book is a solemn warning to every nation that sin can creep back in, however blessed the people were in the past.

Outline of book: Total chapters – 3

- ■ Nahum's visions and warnings – Nineveh will be destroyed (1-2)

- ■ Reasons for the destruction of Nineveh (3)

Habbakuk

A text to remember: **Habakkuk 3:17,18**

Habbakuk was contemporary with Jeremiah. He warns therefore about much the same things, and complains about the wickedness of Judah. God says he will send the Babylonians (Chaldeans) to judge them (see 1:6-11). In 1:13 God is described as "of purer eyes than to behold evil". Habakkuk asks God why it is that a nation even more wicked than Judah will come to judge them (1:12-17).

God tells Habakkuk that the Babylonians will also be judged by him in their turn (chapter 2). It is in this chapter also that we are told the well-known promise, "the just shall live by his faith" (2:4). Habakkuk ends in chapter 3 on a note of absolute trust in God, whatever happens.

How vital it is that we learn to love God even if we face a fearful future: "Although the fig tree shall not blossom..." (3:17-19).

Outline of book: Total chapters – 3

- Habakkuk complains about the sins of God's people (1:1-4)

- God warns them that the Babylonians will come against them (1:5-11)

- Habakkuk looks to God (1:12-17)

- God tells Habakkuk that the Babylonians will be judged also (2)

- Habakkuk's prayer (3:1-16)

- Habakkuk's joy in God, whatever happens (3:17-19)

Zephaniah

A text to remember: **Zephaniah 2:3**

Zephaniah lived at the same time as good king Josiah (see 2 Kings 22 and 23). The book is about the rooting out of idolatry and sin in the land. Chapter 3 describes the rebellion and sin of Jerusalem, and its future judgment. Yet even in this there is hope, for 3:14-17 tells us that God will one day restore Jerusalem again and rejoice over them with singing. One day the people would return to Jerusalem and serve God in purity (3:19,20).

Outline of book: Total chapters – 3

- God's judgments against Judah in the day of the LORD (1:1-2:3)

- God's judgments against the nations in the day of the LORD (2:4-15)

- God's restoration of Jerusalem (3)

Haggai

A text to remember: **Haggai 1:5,6**

To understand this book, we must realise the importance of the temple to Old Testament worship. Neglect of the temple meant neglect of God and His law. The people had become idle and selfish, while the house of God lay in ruins (1:4). Therefore Haggai is called by God to warn them about their wrong priorities. Chapter 1:7,8 reveals that God would take pleasure in the rebuilding of the temple.

Zerubbabel was the king at the time. The temple he built was nowhere near as lavish as the original made by Solomon, but God promised that its *spiritual* glory would be greater (2:3-9).

Outline of book: Total chapters – 2

■ Haggai reproves the people for neglecting God's temple (1)

■ Haggai encourages the people to finish God's temple - blessings present and future (2)

Zechariah

A text to remember: **Zechariah 12:10**

After Isaiah, this prophet has the most to say about the coming Messiah. Zechariah tells us that Jesus is called the Branch (3:8), that He is the king who would one day enter Jerusalem riding upon a donkey (9:9; see Matthew 21:1-5). He also predicts that the Lord Jesus would be sold for 30 pieces of silver (11:13) and that He would be pierced (12:10). Note that the word "me" is used in 12:10. God is speaking in this verse, and it is more evidence that Jesus is divine. Chapter 13:1 tells us about the fountain opened "to the house of David and the inhabitants of Jerusalem for sin and for all uncleanness". This is understood by many to represent the blood of Christ, which washes away all sin.

This book is full of powerful poetic imagery. The prophet speaks about God's protection of His people (2:5) as a "wall of fire" and that whatever is done for God will be achieved, not by might or by power, but by the Spirit of God (4:6). As a matter of interest, although most angels in the Bible appear as men without wings, Zechariah sees angelic beings who appear as women with the "wings of a stork" (5:9). This has for centuries guided the way artists have depicted angels. Zechariah lived at the same time as Haggai, and likewise speaks of the rebuilding of the temple.

Outline of book: Total chapters – 14

- ■ The visions of Zechariah (1-6)
- ■ Zechariah's message to the people (7-8)
- ■ God will save His people (9-14)

Malachi

A text to remember: **Malachi 3:16**

Four centuries separate the end of the Old Testament from the beginning of the New Testament. It is therefore fitting that the last book of the Old Testament should be the last chronologically, and should speak about the coming of Jesus (3:1-4) and the work of the next great prophet, John the Baptist (4:5,6).

The book begins by revealing the hypocrisy of the people. They claim they have honoured God, yet in reality they have despised Him. Chapter 3 deals with their various sins and instructs the people to repent. In 3:8-10 God emphasises the importance of giving a "tithe" (one tenth of everything) to Him. If the people obeyed, God would open the windows of heaven and pour out so much blessing that there would not be enough room to receive it (3:10). In 3:16-18 God calls His people "jewels" and says that a day will come when their hypocrisy will be removed, and they will shine like precious gems.

Outline of book: Total chapters – 4

- ■ Hypocrisy of the people and priests (1-2)
- ■ God's promises to Israel (3-4)

Between the Old and New Testaments

The Old and New Testaments are separated by a time span of about 400 years. Some of this period is described in history and poetry books as the Apocrypha. The Apocrypha was from the beginning regarded as separate from the rest of the Bible, and is not inspired by God. These books must be read with caution. Apocryphal writings speak, for instance, of prayers for the dead, which is nowhere taught in the true word of God.

These books tell us about the days when pagan Greek influences threatened Israel, and wicked leaders, such as Antiochus IV Epiphenes, tried to destroy the worship of God in Jerusalem. The Jews, led by Judas Maccabaeus, bravely resisted, and restored the worship of God.

After a century of Jewish rule, and general peace, history reveals that the year 63BC saw the tide turn. The Romans began to move in. General Pompey attacked Jerusalem, and soon the Romans held sway in Israel. Their rule was bitterly resented by the Jewish people.

In 40 BC Herod was appointed by the Romans as king of Judea. He is known as 'Herod the Great'. It is with this background that the New Testament begins.

Matthew

A text to remember: **Matthew 5:3-5**

Matthew paints a complete picture of the whole life of Jesus Christ. He charts the virgin birth, Jesus' baptism by John the Baptist, Jesus' temptation in the wilderness, His transfiguration, crucifixion, and resurrection. In addition Matthew includes a vivid description of many of Jesus' parables concerning the kingdom of heaven. He tells us too about Jesus' miracles and teachings, as well as pointing out the fulfilment of many Old Testament prophecies written centuries before Jesus was born.

Matthew was a tax collector who was dramatically called to leave his job and follow the Lord Jesus Christ. You can read his own short account of this event in Matthew 9:9 and also a more detailed version in Luke 5:27-31 and Mark 2:14-17. In these latter passages Matthew is referred to by his other name, Levi.

An additional brief guide to Matthew is provided earlier on in this book (p. 9-13).

Outline of book: Total chapters – 28

- Jesus' miraculous birth is described (1-2)

- Jesus' ministry (3-20):
  - His baptism and early popularity (3-4)
  - Sermon on the Mount (5-7)
  - His awesome power over death, disease and nature (8-9)
  - His teachings and opposition from the Pharisees (12-20)

- Jesus' last week in Jerusalem ending in His death by crucifixion (21-27)

- Jesus' resurrection and the great commission (28)

Mark

A text to remember: **Mark 8:35-37**

Mark is a much shorter and more concise book to read than Matthew. Both gospels are very similar, and if you have read Matthew you will recognise many of the events referred to by Mark. Both gospels carefully document the life of Jesus. Mark, however, focuses on the period of Jesus' ministry, death and resurrection and does not mention His birth.

Mark includes a lot more circumstantial detail in his text. He makes it crystal clear that these events actually happened and are accurate. He also chooses to record the events of Jesus' life without referring to Old Testament prophecies so that people who were not of Jewish descent could understand.

Outline of book: Total chapters – 16

- Jesus begins His ministry – baptism and early popularity among the people (1-2)

- Jesus' teachings, parables, miracles and subsequent rejection by the Pharisees (3-10)

- Jesus and the events of the final week in Jerusalem. Death on the cross (11-15)

- Jesus rises from the dead. He sends the disciples to preach to everyone everywhere, and ascends to heaven (16)

Luke

A text to remember: **Luke 4:18,19**

Luke was a doctor (see Colossians 4:14). He had trusted in Jesus Christ as his Saviour, though he was not one of the twelve disciples. He gathered information very carefully, and writes as one who has had a complete understanding of "all things from the very first". He desires every believer to know the *certainty* of what they had been taught (Luke 1:3-4). Luke also wrote the New Testament book of Acts.

As you read this book, you will find that Luke describes many things that Jesus did which are not recorded in the other gospels. For example, read about the young man from Nain who died and was raised to life by Jesus (chapter 7).

Only in Luke will you find the Parables of The Good Samaritan (chapter 10), The Prodigal Son (chapter 15), and The Rich Man and Lazarus (chapter 16). Luke and the other gospels combined show us that Jesus has *absolute power* over man's health, the world we live in, and sin.

Outline of book: Total chapters – 24

- Jesus' birth and childhood described (1-2)
- Jesus begins His ministry (3-5)
- Jesus calls His disciples and teaches in depth (6)
- Jesus continues to show His absolute power, and teaches many parables (7-19:27)
- Jesus' last days in Jerusalem. Jesus dies on the cross (19:28-23)
- Jesus' resurrection and appearance to many disciples. Ascension to heaven (24)

John

A text to remember: **John 3:16**

John was a disciple whom Jesus especially loved. His style of writing is very different from that of Matthew, Mark and Luke. John tells us more about the character and nature of Jesus rather than listing many historical events. If you read the first couple of verses in John 1:1-5, they tell us that Jesus was the "Word". That means that Jesus is the wonderful *expression* of all that God is. Here we find many "I am" sayings of Jesus.

Jesus said:
   "**I am** the Bread of Life" (6:35)
   "**I am** the Light of the World" (8:12)
   "**I am** the Door of the Sheep" (10:7)
   "**I am** the Good Shepherd" (10:11)
   "**I am** the Resurrection, and the Life" (11:25)
   "**I am** the Way, the Truth, and the Life" (14:6)
   "**I am** the True Vine" (15:1)

John wanted people to know that Jesus is the Son of God. He wanted them to have spiritual life by trusting in Him; for that reason this gospel was written (20:31).

Outline of book: Total chapters – 21

■ The identity of Jesus Christ (1)

■ Jesus – The Son of God teaching and healing (2-12)

■ Jesus instructs, warns, and comforts his disciples (13-16)

■ Jesus' prayer (17)

■ Jesus' trial and crucifixion (18-19)

■ Jesus' resurrection and appearance to His disciples by the Sea of Galilee (20-21)

Acts

A text to remember: **Acts 2:38**

Sometimes the title of this book is shortened to "Acts" but its full name is "The Acts of the Apostles". The meaning of the word "apostle" is "sent one". Apostles were therefore people "sent out" to serve the Lord Jesus. It covers the time after Jesus' death when his close followers were frightened and unclear about what they should do. In chapter 2 the Holy Spirit came upon them in great power and their lives were totally transformed. They boldly went forth and told people about Jesus Christ.

The apostles travelled great distances to far away places throughout the known world. The message of the apostles was clear—forgiveness of sins by faith in Christ alone. Their journeys were often dangerous. Paul, an apostle who at one time persecuted Christians, once had to hide in a basket and be let out of a window so that he could escape danger. He experienced beatings, imprisonments, shipwrecks, as well as joy and encouragement during his missionary travels. Paul preached in Turkey, Greece and finally Rome. This book records many other "acts" of Paul and his friends.

Outline of book: Total chapters – 28

■ Life and decisions of the early Christians such as Peter, John, Stephen, and Philip (1-12)

■ Paul's dangerous missionary journeys (13-28):
- *First* – involved Paul, Barnabas and John Mark.
Starting point – Antioch in Syria (13-14)
- *Second* – involved Paul, Silas and Timothy.
Starting point – Antioch in Syria (15:40-ch.18:22)
- *Third* – involved Paul, Timothy and Erastus.
Starting point – Antioch in Syria (18:23-ch. 21:16)
- *Fourth* – involved only Paul who was being sent to Rome for trial.
Starting point – Caesarea (23:23-ch.28)

Romans

A text to remember: **Romans 8:1**

Paul the apostle often wrote letters to the Christians whom he met during his travels. He wrote this letter to Roman believers whom he met during his fourth missionary journey.

Roman Christians were soon to suffer terrible persecution. Here, Paul gives them a solid grounding in the essential truths of the Christian faith. He shows them man's basic sinful nature ("There is none righteous, no, not one" – Romans 3:10-11). He continues by speaking about God's glorious plan of salvation for both Jews

and Gentiles alike. In fact, all who have faith like Abraham are part of God's family (see Romans 3).

This book tells us that God is all-powerful. Chapters 8 and 9 teach that God is sovereign when He saves people from sin, and that all events are under His control. Chapters 10 and 11 speak of God's great plan for His people the Jews.

Outline of book: Total chapters – 16

- God's perspective – on sin (1).

- God's remedy – how we can be saved by faith (2-5)

- God's people – they desire sin no more. They are set free from the punishment and power of sin (6-8)

- God's sovereign plan – of salvation and judgment (9-11)

- God's wisdom – instructions for living a pure Christian life (12-16)

1 Corinthians

A text to remember: **1 Corinthians 13:13**

The group of believers who lived at Corinth in Greece needed a lot of guidance in Christian living. So many disputes and divisions had arisen among them that it threatened the complete break-up of this church. For example there was division of loyalty to the various leaders of the church: Paul, or Apollos, or Cephas? Then there was disorder at the communion table, lawsuits between brethren, as well as immorality that would have been frowned upon even by pagans.

Paul writes to them very sternly concerning their behaviour. It saddened him greatly. He also directs them back to Christ – the solid foundation of every Christian.

He guides them in areas such as marriage, worship, church gatherings, spiritual gifts and the resurrection.

Outline of book: Total chapters – 16

- ■ Trouble threatening church unity – *division* (1-4)

- ■ Trouble concerning the behaviour of church members
  - *immorality and lawsuits* (5-6)

- ■ Teaching relating to specific issues and questions (7-16):
  - marriage (7)
  - food offered to idols (8-10)
  - worship and spiritual gifts (11-14)
  - resurrection (15)
  - collecting for God's people (16:1-4)

2 Corinthians

A text to remember: **2 Corinthians 5:17**

When Paul wrote this second letter to the Corinthians their conduct had vastly improved. Titus had visited them and been able to report that they had changed. They had examined themselves as a group of believers, been sorry for their sins and now were careful in their conduct (chapter 7).

Paul here teaches them about living a holy life. He uses his own apostolic life as an example, revealing his troubles, trials, and ultimately the hopes and promises which sustained him through very difficult situations. Paul also had to defend his call to be an apostle since some Corinthians had complained that he was a weak and unimpressive person (10:10). You can read about the first time Paul went to Corinth in Acts 18:1-18. Paul stayed for one and a half years while travelling on his second missionary journey and worked for a while making tents in order to support his own ministry.

Outline of book: Total chapters – 13

- Paul explains his reasons for not visiting (1-2)
- Paul describes his ministry as an apostle (3-7)
- Paul encourages them to give to the saints (8-9)
- Paul defends his authority as an apostle (10-13)

Galatians

A text to remember: **Galatians 2:16**

Galatia was a vast region that Paul visited many times during his missionary journeys. Paul wrote to the Galatians to "remind" them of the gospel he had once preached to them. They had foolishly forgotten! Inevitably, they were then quickly swayed by false teachers.

One of the more prominent lies that many Galatians believed was that they needed to be circumcised in order to be saved and recognised as members of God's family. They had also been deceived into following the ceremonial washings and sacrifices demanded by Jewish law to deal with sin.

Paul had to tell them all over again how important it is that God's people are saved by *faith* alone in Jesus Christ through God's mercy and kindness. Even Abraham was ultimately justified by *faith* and not by his works. Many of the Jewish laws were only meant to serve as a shadow of the perfection to be achieved by Jesus Christ and were not to be re-established. In fact, this letter is very similar to the first chapters of Romans where our basic sinful nature is outlined and the gift of faith as a pathway to salvation highlighted. Try, for example, looking up and comparing these two verses: Galatians 3:6 and Romans 4:3.

Paul ends by showing the Galatians how to be led by the Holy Spirit. The fruit of the Holy Spirit will be evident in our lives as seen by "love, joy, peace, patience, kindness, goodness, faithfulness, gentleness and self-control" (Galatians 5:22-23).

Outline of book: Total chapters – 6

- Paul makes it clear that God has called him to be a true apostle and to teach the gospel (1-2)

- Paul reminds them of the principles of the gospel. Their freedom in Christ from the law of works (3-5:15)

- Paul teaches them about living a Spirit-filled life. They are a new creation (5:16 - 6:18)

(Map overleaf)   65

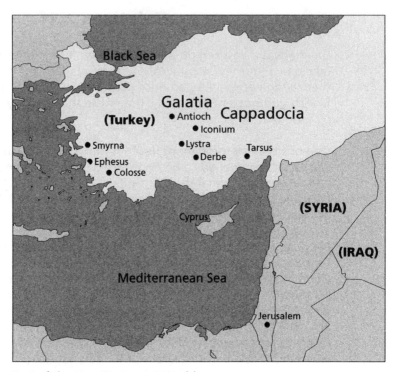

Part of the New Testament World

Ephesians

A text to remember: **Ephesians 2:13**

These Christian believers lived in a very difficult area. Ephesus was the centre of worship for the false goddess Diana.

At Ephesus, the people had built a large temple to worship their idol, as well as a famous theatre where they could sit and be entertained. (Read about Paul's visit here in Acts 19 where a riot soon occurred!).

Paul knew that the Ephesians would face many troubles in the future. He wanted to *encourage* them by recounting God's wonderful grace in saving them. They were now members of God's family built upon the firm foundation of the prophets and apostles with Christ as the chief cornerstone. Paul tells them how to glorify God both in their families and at work (see chapters 4 and 5). This theme we find again in Colossians. He also paints a picture of *preparation and reliance upon God's strength* in his closing comments.

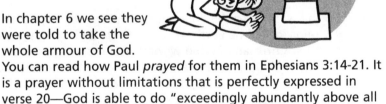

In chapter 6 we see they were told to take the whole armour of God. You can read how Paul *prayed* for them in Ephesians 3:14-21. It is a prayer without limitations that is perfectly expressed in verse 20—God is able to do "exceedingly abundantly above all that we ask or think" according to His power.

Outline of book: Total chapters – 6

- God's grace saves the Ephesians (1-2)
- Paul prays for the Ephesians (3)
- Paul teaches them about unity in the Holy Spirit and practical Christian living (4-6)

Philippians

A text to remember: **Philippians 1:21**

The Philippians were very dear to Paul. It was in Philippi that Paul and his friend Silas had been in prison. An earthquake sent by God set them free. Their jailer had wanted to kill himself and was later saved. Another famous believer in Philippi was Lydia, the seller of purple cloth, whose heart had been opened by God to listen to Paul. You can read about them in Acts 16:12-40.

The Philippian church had always been faithful in supporting Paul in his work for God. Yet Paul's circumstances appeared desperate and bleak when he wrote this letter. He had been imprisoned and placed under guard for preaching the gospel. Despite his surroundings, Paul realised that God would use this time in chains to further the spread of the gospel (1:15-30).

In his letter to the Philippians, Paul speaks frequently about *rejoicing* in the Lord. This was to be an important part of their Christian life and witness. He also teaches them to be Christ-like in humility and love, and united in purpose.

Outline of book: Total chapters – 4

- ■ Paul explains his situation, and talks about what has caused him to rejoice (1)

- ■ Christ's people – are to be like Jesus in love, humility and unity (2)

- ■ Christ's people – need to beware of false doctrine and be steadfast in the faith (3)

- ■ Paul's final exhortations and greetings (4)

Colossians

A text to remember: **Colossians 1:16,17**

Paul had never met the Colossian believers personally (see 2:1). However, he had heard good news of their Christian example and love. Paul writes to instruct this young church. This letter teaches us principally about the character and greatness of Jesus Christ. Christ is the *image* of the invisible God and by Him all things were created. Christ is seated at the right hand of God and has supremacy in everything. He is in essence our creator and redeemer. If we say that we know Jesus then we should be like a "new" person who obeys His teachings (Colossians 3:9-10).

Paul also tells those at Colosse many other things about Christian doctrine and living. It is similar to Ephesians where Paul points out how parents, wives, husbands and children should behave toward each other. Compare Colossians 3:18-21 and Ephesians 5 and 6.

Outline of book: Total chapters – 4

- Paul's prayers and thanks to God for the Colossians (1:1-14)
- Jesus Christ – who He is and what He has done (1:15-23)
- Paul describes the purpose of his ministry (1:24-ch.2:5)
- Jesus Christ – how His people should obey Him (2:6-ch.4)

1 Thessalonians

A text to remember: **1 Thess. 4:16-18**

When Paul came to the city of Thessalonica many of the devout Greeks became Christians. Some of the Jews, however, formed a lynch mob and set out to capture him. Look up Acts 17:1-14 to read about this incident.

Paul wrote two separate letters to the Thessalonians. Both of these letters centre on the theme of Christ's second coming. Such a day would come upon people suddenly – like a "thief in the night" (5:2).
The Thessalonians were therefore to prepare themselves by living holy lives. They were also to be comforted by the fact of the resurrection of the dead and life in heaven with Christ.

Outline of book: Total chapters – 5

- ■ Paul's prayers and thanks to God for the Thessalonians (1)

- ■ Paul summarises his ministry to the Thessalonians (2-3)

- ■ Paul exhorts them to holiness and preparation for Jesus' return (4-5)

2 Thessalonians

A text to remember: **2 Thessalonians 2:3**

When Paul wrote this second letter he could commend the Thessalonians for their increase in faith despite a great deal of persecution. However there was still misunderstanding about the imminent day of Christ's return. How would they know when these events were to happen? Perhaps Christ had already returned and there was no point in working at all. Paul clarifies the situation by telling them that one sign would be the appearance of the "wicked one" or Antichrist. He must come *before* Christ's Second Coming.

Outline of book: Total chapters – 3

■ Paul encourages their growth in faith despite persecution (1)

■ Paul teaches them about Jesus' return – a clarification (2)

■ Paul asks for prayer and warns against laziness (3)

1 Timothy

A text to remember: **1 Timothy 6:6-8**

The title of the next 3 books – Timothy, Titus and Philemon are the names of individuals rather than gatherings of believers. Paul had something special to say to each one, and we ourselves learn a great deal from them.

Timothy was a young Christian who was learning to become a teacher and preacher of God's Word. Despite his youth, he would have many responsibilities involving church leadership and discipline, faithfully preaching God's Word and caring for others. Paul in this letter gives Timothy many instructions. He was taught, for example, about the qualifications that elders and deacons should have in order to be faithful church leaders (chapter 3). In 1 Thessalonians 3 we read about Timothy encouraging the Thessalonians and then reporting back to Paul.

Outline of book: Total chapters – 6

- The challenge of the ministry – a war between truth and error (1)

- Guidelines for public worship and appointing church leaders (2-3)

- Timothy is warned and instructed as a Christian leader (4-6):
  - beware false teachers (4)
  - handling particular groups of people (5)
  - pursuit of godliness (6)

2 Timothy

A text to remember: **2 Timothy 4:7,8**

This letter is thought to be the last, chronologically, that the apostle Paul wrote. Chapter 4 tells us about many people who had deserted Paul in his hour of need. It is believed by many that Paul was soon to be executed by the vicious Roman Emperor Nero. Here he writes to warn and instruct those left behind.

Paul particularly warns Timothy to be faithful and strong through the grace of Jesus Christ. There would be times of suffering and hardship ahead for Timothy. In fact, Paul warns that "everyone who wants to live a godly life in Christ Jesus will be persecuted" (3:12).

Paul's final word for Timothy is: "Preach the Word; be prepared in season and out of season; correct, rebuke and encourage – with great patience and careful instruction" (4:2).

Paul tells us towards the end of the letter that he has "fought the good fight", "finished the race" and "kept the faith", and will receive as his reward from the Lord a crown of righteousness (2 Timothy 4:7-8).

Outline of book: Total chapters – 4

- Timothy – must be strong and steadfast (1-2)
- Timothy – told of dangerous times ahead and false teachers (3)
- Timothy – told of great trials which Paul had to endure; but also of God's faithfulness (4)

Titus

A text to remember: **Titus 2:11,12**

Titus, whose name means "honourable", was a Christian sent by Paul to the island of Crete in the Mediterranean Sea. Here he was to help teach the believers and organise their churches, just like Timothy.

In chapter 1 Paul speaks of the holiness God requires for church leaders. But in case the rest of us feel we can live as we like, chapter 2 tells us how people in all walks of life can serve God. Look up Titus 3:1-2 and notice how different God's way is from the world around us.

Outline of book: Total chapters – 3

- Guidelines for appointing church leaders (1)
- Instructions for teaching particular groups of people in the church (2)
- Further guidance for Titus as a teacher (3)

Philemon

A text to remember: **Philemon v. 4,5**

This New Testament book is only 1 chapter long and is the shortest letter that we have that was written by Paul. It focuses on the story of one man called Onesimus, who had run away from his master, Philemon.

Onesimus became a Christian after meeting Paul in Rome. Paul wrote this letter to ask Philemon to *forgive* Onesimus and to receive him as a brother in Christ.

Outline of book: Total chapters – 1

- ■ Paul's prayer and thanks to God for Philemon (vv. 1-7)
- ■ Paul's appeal for Onesimus (vv. 8-21)
- ■ Paul's final request and greetings (vv. 22-25)

Hebrews

A text to remember: **Hebrews 10:11,12**

No one knows for sure who wrote this book, possibly Paul, although we are not told the author. What is certain is that he had a deep knowledge of the Old Testament, and was shown by God how the scriptures point to the Lord Jesus. The writer is particularly speaking to "Hebrews", that is to Jewish people, and teaches that Jesus is central to all the Old Testament laws and ceremonies. Jesus is much *greater* than Moses, Abraham, or indeed any of the Old Testament prophets. He is the promised "Christ", the Son of God whose throne will last forever and ever, one whom all of God's angels worship. The writer of course tells us much more about Jesus Christ and explains just how His death has brought salvation to all who believe in Him.

This letter was written particularly to Jewish Christians. It therefore makes many references to Old Testament characters such as Abraham and Moses, and scriptures which would be familiar to Jewish people.

Chapter 11 of Hebrews is particularly well known and lists many men and women of faith from the Old Testament.

Outline of book: Total chapters – 13

- ■ Christ – His majesty and exalted position (1-2)
- ■ Christ – our High Priest (3-7)
- ■ Christ – perfects the first covenant with Israel (8-10)
- ■ Examples of faith from Israel's past, encouragements for the future (11-12)
- ■ Practical teachings for a pure and holy Christian life (13)

James

A text to remember: **James 1:27**

The next 3 books that we come to in the New Testament (James, Peter and John) were written by Jesus' disciples and named after them. Look up Matthew 10:1-4 to find the names of all 12 disciples. You will notice that there were two disciples named James. (The James that wrote this particular letter was probably James the son of Alphaeus).

One reason James wrote this letter was to teach believers about their faith in God. It was a faith that should express itself practically by caring for others. Faith and good deeds are to go together; neither should stand alone. Otherwise both are useless and dead. Put simply, our deeds reveal whether our faith is genuine or not. James here gives a wealth of advice on other matters as well. In chapter 3, for example, he particularly warns about the dangers of an uncontrolled tongue. Such a small part of our bodies can be just as lethal as a blazing fire.

Outline of book: Total chapters – 5

- ■ Practical guidelines for the Christian (1-2):
  - trials and temptations (1:2-18)
  - hypocrisy (1:19-27)
  - favouritism (2:1-13)
  - faith and works (2:14-26)

- ■ Focus on self-control and the tongue (3)

- ■ More practical guidelines for the Christian (4-5):
  - godliness (4:1-12)
  - boasting (4:13-17)
  - riches (5:1-6)
  - patience (5:7-12)
  - prayer (5:13-18)

1 Peter

A text to remember: **1 Peter 2:7**

Peter is one of the few disciples who was with Jesus on important occasions such as the raising of Jairus' daughter, the transfiguration and His prayer in the garden of Gethsemane. Peter's original name was Simon. His name in the Aramaic language is "Cephas". Both "Peter" and "Cephas" mean a stone or rock.

There are two letters written by Peter, both of which are written to Christians living in many different countries. Peter wanted them to always *remember* what they had been taught. We so easily forget! In this first letter Peter reminds believers that they "are a chosen people, a royal priesthood, a holy nation." (2:9). They were to be holy in all aspects of their lives. They were also to be ready for the attacks of the devil who is compared to a prowling lion (1 Peter 5:8).

Outline of book: Total chapters – 5

- God the Father – His mercy and power in salvation is praised (1:1-12)

- Christians are to live holy lives (1:13-ch.2:12)

- Teaching for particular people within the church (2:13-ch.3:7)

- Christians and suffering (3:8-ch.5:14)

2 Peter

A text to remember: **2 Peter 1:10**

Peter again makes it a priority to *remind* believers in Christ of certain gospel truths. Namely, God has given us great and precious promises by which we can indeed live holy lives and make our calling and election sure. Even though we have the sure and trustworthy Word of God, there will certainly be many false teachers whose errors we must reject.

Peter was an "eye-witness" of the glory of Jesus Christ and as such assures them that they have not followed cleverly invented fables. Peter emphasises the truth and authority of the Old Testament (1:19-21).

Additionally, Peter reminds believers of the end of the age and the coming of Jesus Christ (2 Peter 3:10). They should be prepared by making every effort to be found "spotless, blameless and at peace with him" (3:14).

Outline of book: Total chapters – 3

- Peter encourages believers to grow in the faith (1)
- Peter describes and warns against false teachers (2)
- Peter reminds believers of the certainty of Jesus' coming (3)

1 John

A text to remember: **1 John 1:8,9**

John was another of the 12 disciples; he was one of Jesus' closest companions. He is the same person that wrote the gospel of John and describes the Lord Jesus as the "Word".

In his letters you will find that John refers to the young Christians as "little children". He simply wanted believers to know *how* they could tell if they were really Christians or not. If they said, for example, that they loved God, then they should also love their brother and hate sin. John identifies three marks of a true Christian: that they believe God, that they obey God, and that they love their fellow brothers and sisters in Christ.

John also speaks of "antichrists" as people who show by their actions that they hate Jesus. He uses the words *love, hate, darkness* and *light* many times, to draw a contrast between those who love God and those who do not.

Outline of book: Total chapters – 5

■ John speaks of the glory of Jesus Christ (1:1-4)

■ John describes true Christian holiness (1:5-ch.5)

2 John

A text to remember: **2 John v. 6**

Here John describes himself simply as "the elder" and writes this letter to the "chosen lady and her children". This may simply be a reference to a household of believers or individuals who were not to be identified due to persecution.

John speaks of the encouragement that these Christians had been to him and reminds them to love one another. In addition they were to beware of "deceivers" who did not continue in the teachings of Jesus Christ. Such false teachers were not even to be received into their homes (vv. 10,11).

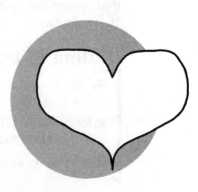

Outline of book: Total chapters – 1

■ John's joy in the believers of the church. They are to show love and to obey God (vv. 1-6)

■ John warns believers about false teachers. They are not to be welcomed (vv. 7-11)

■ John's desire to visit. Final greetings (vv. 12-13)

∃ John

A text to remember: **3 John v. 4**

In this letter John writes to a fellow believer named Gaius. Gaius is encouraged in his fellowship and love for other believers. By contrast, Diotrephes is a man to be avoided for his pride and wickedness within the church. John reminds us that we are not to imitate evil, and whoever practises it has "not seen God" (v. 11).

Outline of book: Total chapters – 1

- John encourages Gaius in his faithfulness and love towards others (vv. 1-8)

- John rebukes Diotrephes for gossip, pride and maliciousness (vv. 9-11)

- John commends Demetrius. Final greetings (vv. 12-13)

Jude

A text to remember: **Jude v. 3**

Some believe that Jude was a half-brother of the Lord Jesus, referred to at the end of a list in Matthew 13:55. Whoever the author may be, his aim was to warn all those that trust in Jesus Christ to *beware* of false disciples. He wanted them to fight for the faith they had received. It is a short letter, only 1 chapter, and it tells us that people will enter the church *pretending* to be Christians. They will spread error and act in an ungodly way.

God will overcome and punish their evil actions just as he destroyed the cities of Sodom and Gomorrah in the Old Testament. In verses 5 and 6 we read of two other examples of God's swift judgment upon the ungodly. It is very similar to 2 Peter 2.

Outline of book: Total chapters – 1

- Christians are to defend the truth (vv. 1-4)

- Examples of God's swift judgment (vv. 5-10)

- How false Christians will behave (vv. 11-19)

- How true Christians are to live (vv. 20-25)

Revelation

A text to remember: **Revelation 21:4**

This book is unique among the books of the New Testament because it predicts in detail future judgments. These judgments occur in three main groups. There are "seal" judgments, each one occurring as a seal on a scroll is opened. These are followed by "trumpet" judgments, which occur as seven trumpets are blown, and finally "bowl or vial" judgments, poured out as seven bowls are emptied.

Each set of judgments is worse than before, as God gradually increases the severity of His punishments for sin. Compare for instance the second trumpet judgment (8:8) with the second bowl judgment (16:3).

You will notice that a third of sea creatures are destroyed in the first passage, and every single one in the second. This gradual increase in punishment teaches us that God gives us time and opportunity to repent, but few people take Him seriously and listen to His warnings. In fact, for some, the judgments of God make them only bitter, and they cry out in anger against God (see 16:10,11 and 21).

This book tells us of the end of all evil and the "passing away" of planet earth as we know it today. It tells us of a "new heaven and new earth" that will be prepared only for God's people to enjoy. As such, it is called the book of Revelation since it "reveals" to us this sequence of events. The original name for this book is Apokalupsis, or Apocalypse, meaning "to take the veil away from" events yet unseen. Some of the events depicted here have occurred already (see chapter 12). Others will occur *before, during,* and *after* Jesus returns from heaven.

In this book there are a lot of numbers, imagery, and symbols. Notice, for example, how often the numbers 7 and 12 are used. The important thing to know, however, is that God wants us *to be prepared* for the return of His Son. That is why He will send lots of signs and warnings to remind us. God told these things to John the disciple in a vision so that he would keep and *remember* them. This book promises special blessings to all who study and love it (see Revelation 1:1-3).

Outline of book: Total chapters – 22

- John's vision and warning to the 7 churches of Asia (1-3)

- John's vision of heaven and the seal/trumpet judgments (4-11)

- John's vision of specific events concerning the end times (12-14)

- John's vision of the 7 angels and the vial (bowl) judgments (15-16)

- John's vision of specific events during the last days (17-18)

- John's vision of a triumphant new heaven and earth, and the judgment of Satan (19-22)

Studying the Bible

Pray first

The Bible is no ordinary Book. It is the Word of God. As such it should not be merely read and studied as literature, or coldly analysed.

John Bunyan, the Bedfordshire tinker who wrote *Pilgrim's Progress,* left us an excellent example of Bible study in his life. For Bunyan, the Bible was no mere textbook, or intriguing document; it was God's voice to men and women. It made him rejoice; it also made him at times weep and cry out, asking God for mercy. It was a living book to him.

Many Christians of the past, such as John Bradford the martyr and George Müller, read the Bible on their knees. This is not essential by any means, but it conveys far more the attitude we should have when we read than simply the picture of a cold-hearted student sitting in a library.

Study of the Bible should therefore be prayerful. Pray before you read that God will help you to obey what it says and to take its warnings to heart.

Approaching a passage

When you come to any part of the Bible ask, what are the circumstances of these verses? What is actually said or done? What did this mean to the first people who heard and saw these things? What does it mean to me now?

Here is an example. In John 8:58 Jesus said, "Before Abraham was, I am." Now Jesus was in the temple area, surrounded by Jews who knew the Old Testament. He says, "Before Abraham was, I am". Not, you notice, "I had existence" or "I knew I would come", but, "I am". The original Greek, "ego aime" can only mean "I am". Jesus is using the same words that we find in Exodus 3:14, where Jehovah God says, "I am that I am". Jesus was saying therefore that He had equal power and glory with Jehovah God.

What about the context? Is this how the Jews understood it? How did they react? The next verse reads, "then took they up stones to cast at Him". Stoning was the punishment for blasphemy. Thus Jesus was indeed identifying Himself with Jehovah God, and their reaction confirms that this was the case.

Making Notes

It is good to make notes. Some choose a Bible with sufficient space in the margin to allow for notes next to the text itself. Others choose to write in a separate book or sheet of paper. The missionary CT Studd made regular notes in his Bible, but bought a new copy each year, so that as he read it his mind would *not* follow previous lines of thought, but be given fresh insight.

It is good to read the Bible right through. We have recommended beginning with the New Testament and then reading the Old Testament. It is easily possible to read the Bible through once each year, but it takes determination and, most importantly of all, a sense of the supreme importance of this task. If the Bible is God's Word, surely it deserves first place among the books we read.

It is helpful to mark your Bible with useful information and other references as you hear sermons and read Christian books. When the apostle Paul preached in Thessalonica, the people from nearby Berea "searched the scriptures daily" to see whether what he taught was according to the scriptures (Acts 17:11). To listen with an inquiring mind is a virtue. It is very helpful to write down questions to ask your pastor or church leader. No question is foolish if you genuinely want to know the answer. "Do animals go to heaven?" "What is heaven like?" "Why were there so many wars in the Old Testament?" These and other questions are answered by the Bible, so use the wealth of Christian knowledge and understanding of the Bible in people around you.

Background information, and notes on the original meaning of words are all useful in Bible study. Merely underlining or highlighting a verse is not as helpful as writing notes beside it. Why have you highlighted it? What verses elsewhere follow a similar theme? How does this speak to you today? etc. By making regular notes, you will be amazed just how much of the Bible will become familiar to you in a short space of time.

Bible Meditation

It is very important to meditate upon the Word of God. This means to prayerfully consider and devote your mind to a passage of scripture. It helps to think about the verse or group of verses as they relate to every aspect of life. Psalm 1:2,3 speaks about the blessings that come to those who meditate upon the Bible. It makes a Christian really fruitful spiritually.

Paul instructed Timothy to meditate on what he had been taught (1 Timothy 4:15). Some people study a verse or two deeply each day. These may be part of the few pages you read that morning, or else a verse or two from a different book. Psalm 119 for instance is perfect for meditating upon a verse or two each day. The New Testament letters such as Colossians and 1 and 2 Peter are an excellent place to start. Thus, you may wish to study a longer passage as part of your daily reading, and then take a verse or two for particular meditation. Some write these few verses on a piece of paper and take it with them through the day. Whenever there is an opportunity, they seek to memorise and study this short passage from the Bible. It is amazing how precious and relevant the Word of God will become for you as you meditate in this way.

Talk about the Bible

God commanded His people to read and talk about His Word all the time. If the Bible is truly the Word of God to us, then we must not neglect it. Christians should make it not just a *part* of their lives, but their chief delight wherever they go; read carefully Deuteronomy 6:6,7.

To summarise:

1. Pray first. God gave us the Bible and He is the best guide; so ask Him to help you to understand it. We must come to the Bible not only to be *challenged* by it, but to be *changed* by it. It should affect the way we think and behave at home, at school, and at work.

2. Approach the passage carefully. Try not to hurry, but read it with care, thinking about what the passage teaches, finding out background information from a Bible dictionary or commentary and looking at how it relates to other passages elsewhere in the Bible.

3. Take a pen when you read, and note down any questions or thoughts you have as you read. There are pages at the end of this book for some notes. Show some questions to your pastor or church leader, who I am sure will be keen to help you.

4. Meditate upon what you read. Think about what the Bible has said to you. Pray as you read and re-read a section of the Bible.

5. Talk about the Bible. Don't waste time talking about trivial things. Read the Bible eagerly and talk about it every day.

Helpful Tools

We have found that the following books would really help you to understand the Bible:

i. A Bible dictionary.

This book, especially if it is well illustrated, can give you real insight into Bible people, places and customs. Make sure though, that the writers believe the Word of God and are not going to mislead you. This is true of any book you read about the Bible.

Baker's Bible Dictionary: A Bible Dictionary that gives the history of Israel, fills in the background of the Bible and is an excellent tool in understanding the Word of God. Who were the Ammonites and Philistines? Where is Babylon? Look no further!

ii. A Concordance.

This gives you lists of words and where to find them in the Bible. It helps you find verses if you are not sure where to look for them.

Strong's Exhaustive Concordance: Sometimes you will recall part of a verse, but not where it is found in the Bible. This is when to use a concordance. An "exhaustive" one merely means it lists every single word from the Bible, including every "and" and "at"!

Nave's Topical Bible: This book lists Bible verses under various themes and headings. Many of the verses are written out in full. This is a great help to studying the Bible subject by subject.

iii. Commentaries.

These explain parts of the Bible verse by verse. The best way to use them is to pray as you read the Bible passage on its own, then write down your own thoughts and *lastly* study the commentary. Too often these books are used as a *replacement* for our own prayerful thoughts. Remember that the Bible is no ordinary book. Its Author is only a prayer away.

Matthew Henry's Commentary: This may take a little more saving to obtain! However, we think it is most helpful since he not only explains the Bible, but also shows in a practical way how it should affect our lives. Although some of the language is quaint it is regarded as one of the best Bible commentaries of all time.

Finally...

Some passages in the Bible to look up...

When you are Seeking God...
Isaiah 55:6,7; Acts 2:38,39; 16:29-31

For those who already trust in Christ...

When you are:

Angry . . . . Ephesians 4:26-32

Anxious . . . . Isaiah 26:3; Philippians 4:6,7

Backsliding . . . . 1 Kings 8:46-52

Bereaved . . . . Job 1:18-22

Confused . . . . 2 Chronicles 20:12; Proverbs 3:5,6

Depressed . . . . Psalms13 and 42

Doubting . . . . 1 Thess 2:13; 2 Peter 1:16-21

Far from God . . . . Isaiah 53:6

Fearful . . . . Psalm 27:1-6

Full of Guilt . . . . Psalm 51; 1 John 1:8,9

Heartbroken . . . . Psalm 147:3; Luke 4:18,19

Ill . . . . Lamentations 3:22-40; James 5:14-16

Joyful . . . . Psalms 100; 126; 148

Let down by Others . . . Psalm 27:9,10; 2 Timothy 4:16,17

Lonely . . . . Psalm 73:25; Matthew 28:19,20

Needing Guidance . . . . Psalm 119:105

Spiritually Dry . . . . Job 23:8-10

Stressed . . . . 2 Corinthians 11:22-30

Suffering Financially . . Psalm 50:9,10; Matthew 6:24-34

Weak . . . . 2 Corinthians 12:9,10

Your Bible questions and notes